Materials

Rubber

Chris Oxlade

www.heinemann.co.uk/library
Visit our website to find out more information about **Heinemann Library** books.

To Order:
☎ Phone 44 (0) 1865 888066
▤ Send a fax to 44 (0) 1865 314091
💻 Visit the Heinemann Library Bookshop at www.heinemann.co.uk/library to browse
our catalogue and order online.

First published in Great Britain by Heinemann Library, Halley Court, Jordan Hill, Oxford OX2 8EJ
a division of Reed Educational and Professional Publishing Ltd.
Heinemann is a registered trademark of Reed Educational & Professional Publishing Ltd.

OXFORD MELBOURNE AUCKLAND JOHANNESBURG BLANTYRE
GABORONE IBADAN PORTSMOUTH (NH) USA CHICAGO

Designed by Storeybooks
Originated by Ambassador Litho Ltd.
Printed and bound in Hong Kong/China

ISBN 0 431 12736 0
06 05 04 03 02
10 9 8 7 6 5 4 3 2 1

British Library Cataloguing in Publication Data
Oxlade, Chris
Rubber. – (Materials)
1.Rubber – Juvenile literature
I.Title
620.1'94

Acknowledgements
The Publishers would like to thank the following for permission to reproduce photographs:
Chapel Studios: pp10, 20, 23, 24, 25; Dennis Day: p19; Ecoscene: Stephen Coyne p22, Lorenzo Lees p14,
Christine Osborne p4; Eye Ubiquitous: p17; GSF Picture Library: p21; Hodder Wayland: p7; Martyn
Chillmaid: p6; Panos: Chris Stowers p11; Roger Scruton: p8; Science Photo Library: pp12, 16, 18, 26, 29;
Still Pictures: p27; TRH Pictures: p15; Trip: I Kolpakova p13; Tudor Photography: pp5, 9.

Cover photograph reproduced with permission of Trevor Clifford.

Every effort has been made to contact copyright holders of any material reproduced in this book.
Any omissions will be rectified in subsequent printings if notice is given to the Publisher.

Contents

You can find words shown in bold, **like this,** in the Glossary.

What is rubber?

Rubber is a bendy material. Some rubber is **natural**. It comes from trees. Some rubber is made from **chemicals**. These sheets of rubber are waiting to be made into other objects.

Rubber is a very useful material.
We make many different objects from
it, from car tyres to rubber gloves.
All the objects shown
here are made
from rubber.

Stretchy and strong

Rubber bands are made of rubber. If you stretch a rubber band and then let go, it springs back into shape. This is because rubber is an **elastic** material.

Some types of rubber are soft, like the rubber in a pencil eraser. Some types of rubber are much harder. This **conveyor belt** is made of hard, strong rubber.

More properties of rubber

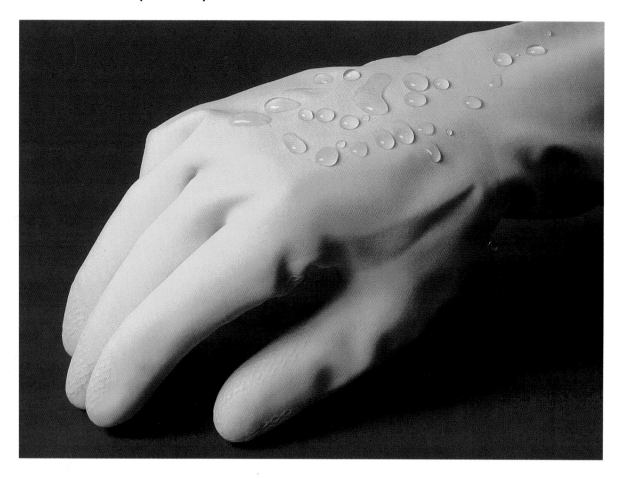

If you pour water on a piece of rubber, the water runs off. Water does not soak into rubber because rubber is **waterproof**. So rubber can be used to keep things dry.

Have you ever tried sliding a piece of rubber along a table? It doesn't slide easily. This is because rubber has a soft **surface** that **grips** the table top.

Natural rubber

Natural rubber comes from rubber trees. The rubber is in the sticky **sap** of the tree. A worker cuts slits in the tree trunk. Then the sap runs into a cup.

The sap has tiny bits of rubber in it.
Chemicals are added to the sap to
make the rubber bits clump together.
The clumps of rubber are rolled to
make sheets.

Rubber from oil

Most of the rubber we use today is made in **factories**. It is made from **chemicals** which come from oil. Oil is found under the sea and in the ground.

Some of the chemicals in oil are
taken out and sent to a factory.
They are mixed with other chemicals
to make rubber. This is a factory
which makes rubber.

Rubber tyres

Tyres for bicycles and cars are made of rubber. The rubber is heated until it melts. Then it is poured into a container shaped like a tyre. When the rubber has cooled, a new tyre comes out.

Rubber tyres **grip** ground well. They are made of hard rubber so they last a long time. The pattern of grooves on a tyre is called the tread.

Stretching and bouncing

Lots of things are made from rubber because rubber can stretch. Party balloons are made of rubber. When you blow up a party balloon, it stretches to ten times its original size!

Rubber is good for making things that bounce. Tennis balls are made of two pieces of rubber, glued together. Golf balls are also made of rubber.

Rubber for clothes

Rubber is good for making **waterproof** clothes. Some clothes are made from **fabric** covered in rubber. Wellington boots are made by dipping a boot shape in hot, runny rubber.

Surfers and divers wear wetsuits when the water is cold. Wetsuits must fit tightly. They are made of a special thick, stretchy rubber fabric.

Gripping with rubber

Rubber makes things easier to **grip**.
The handle on this hammer is covered
with rubber. It stops the hammer
slipping out of your hand.

This rock climber is wearing boots
with rubber soles that grip the rock.
They help to keep her safe. A washing
machine stands on rubber feet. The
feet stop it sliding about.

Rubber tubes

Rubber can be made into long, bendy tubes. The rubber is melted and squeezed through a ring-shaped hole. A garden hose is a long rubber tube. Water travels along the tube to where it is needed.

The black rubber strips on this window are called **seals**. Rubber seals make a tight join around things. When the window is shut the seals stop wind and rain getting in.

Foam rubber

Foam rubber is a squashy material. It is made by blowing air into hot, runny rubber. Inside the foam rubber are millions of tiny air bubbles that can squash down.

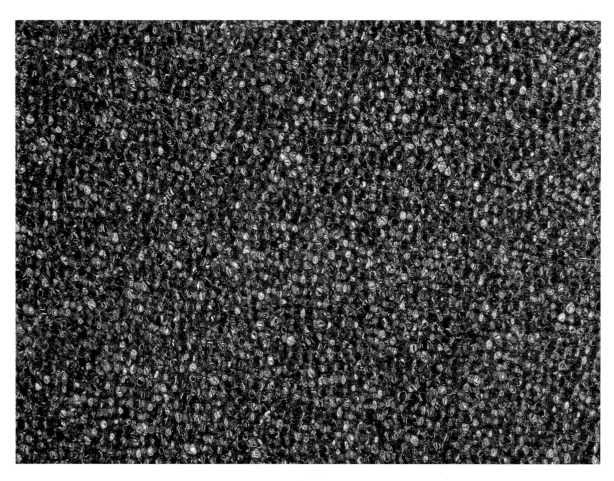

Many chairs, sofas and mattresses have thick sheets of foam rubber inside. Foam rubber is also used for protecting things that could break.

Getting rid of rubber

Every day, millions of worn-out car tyres
are thrown away. They are difficult to get
rid of because rubber does not **rot** away.
Rubber cannot be burned because it
makes nasty black smoke.

Rubber can be used again, or **recycled**. Rubber from old tyres is chopped into bits and mixed with new rubber. Then it can be used to make new things, like these sandles.

Fact file

- Some rubber is **natural**. It comes from the **sap** of rubber trees.

- Some rubber is made in **factories**.

- Rubber can be soft and stretchy.

- Rubber can also be made hard and strong.

- Rubber is **waterproof**.

- Rubber is good at **gripping** things.

- Rubber burns when it is heated.

- Rubber does not let electricity flow through it.

- Rubber is not attracted by magnets.

Would you believe it?

Rubber is used to make monster tyres for diggers and dumper trucks. The largest rubber tyres ever made are 3.8 metres high. That's twice as tall as an adult!

Glossary

chemicals   special materials that are used in factories and homes to do many jobs, including cleaning

conveyor belt   very long, wide sheet of rubber that moves along carrying objects from one place to another

elastic   material that can be stretched or squashed easily, and goes back to its original shape afterwards

fabric   woven or knitted material, such as cloth

factory   place where things are made using machines

foam   soft material that is full of air bubbles

grip   to hold on firmly

natural comes from plants, animals or the rocks in the Earth

recycle to use a material again

rot be eaten away by tiny animals and plants in the ground

sap liquid inside the trunk of a tree

seal rubber strip around the edge of a door or window that stops air and water getting through

surface the very outside of an object

waterproof does not let water pass through

More books to read

Images: Materials and Their Properties
Big Book Compilation
Heinemann Library, 1999

My World of Science
Angela Royston
Heinemann Library, 2001

New Star Science: Materials and Their Uses
Ginn, 2001

Science All Around Me: Materials
Karen Bryant-Mole
Heinemann Library, 1996

Index

Titles in the *Materials* series include:

Hardback   0 431 12737 9

Hardback   0 431 12738 7

Hardback   0 431 12736 0

Hardback   0 431 12735 2

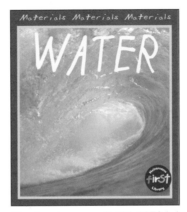

Hardback   0 431 12734 4

Find out about the other titles in this series on our website www.heinemann.co.uk/library